T5-CVP-907

Copyright © 2013 Jo Meserve Mach
All rights reserved.
ISBN: 1494793652
ISBN 13: 9781494793654
Library of Congress Control Number: 2013923765
CreateSpace Independent Publishing Platform, North Charleston, SC

I Want To Be Like Poppin' Joe

Finding My Way Books

true stories of inclusion and
the development of skills
needed for self-determination

By Jo Meserve Mach and
Vera Lynne Stroup-Rentier
Photography by Mary Birdsell

A True Story
Promoting Self-Determination

I'm Dylan and this is Poppin' Joe.
He's my friend.

He likes to clean cars. He likes to fill cups.
He likes to be with his dad.
He likes to juggle. He likes to be busy.

He had to decide what he liked best.
He picked making popcorn with his dad.
It keeps him busy. Now that's his job.

I like to play with my dog. I like to give hugs.
I like to be with my dad. I like to dig.
I like to be outside.

Poppin' Joe learned how to make popcorn.
He knows how to mix corn, sugar, and oil.
He knows just the right parts.

This is what I like to mix.
I can be like Poppin' Joe.

Poppin' Joe weighs sugar.
He knows how much to use.

I can weigh plants.
I can be like Poppin' Joe.

Poppin' Joes knows how to listen.
Pop, pop, pop, pop..pop...pop....pop.
He knows when the popcorn is done.

I listen to Dad. He tells me how to plant.
I can be like Poppin' Joe.

Poppin' Joe knows how much salt to use.
He counts the shakes of salt it needs.

I can count plants. I count 1, 2, 3.
I can be like Poppin' Joe.

Poppin' Joe knows when to dump popcorn.

I can dump dirt.
I can be like Poppin' Joe.

Poppin' Joe knows how to rake popcorn.
He helps it cool down.

I can rake.
I can be like Poppin' Joe.

Poppin' Joe knows how to shovel popcorn into bags. He puts it into bags to sell.

I can shovel dirt.
I can be like Poppin' Joe.

Poppin' Joe know how to load popcorn.

I can load plants.
I can be like Poppin' Joe.

Poppin' Joe knows how to sell his popcorn.
He gets money.

I get money for working in the yard.
I can be like Poppin' Joe.

Poppin' Joe knows how to work hard.

I work hard helping my Dad.
I can be like Poppin' Joe.

Poppin' Joe likes what he decided to do.
He's the boss.

Someday, I'll decide what I like to do best.

Someday, I'm going to be the boss.
I want to be like Poppin' Joe.

Thank you to Dylan and Joe's families
for sharing their stories

Family Guide for Promoting Self-Determination

Cultivate your child's interests:

This story shares many of Joe and Dylan's interests. Joe's parents followed his interests as they explored a variety of volunteer and job opportunities for Joe. These included vacuuming at the church, doing yard work, and being part of the maintenance crew for a community swimming pool. Dylan's parents provide Dylan with many opportunities to be outside. He works with Dad, plays with his brother, Jacob, and plays with the family dog. He also likes to help his Mom when she bakes.

Build on your child's strengths:

Joe's strengths include being a hard worker, pleasing people by doing what he is asked to do, liking order or neatness, laughing and have a good time. It was important to Joe's parents that his job builds on all these strengths. The Kettle Korn business requires him to work hard, to keep the booth organized and neat, to be with many people, and allows him to have a good time with his family and co-workers.

Dylan has wonderful strengths. He loves to laugh and tease people. He is a great hugger. He is good at convincing others to do things by telling them to "try it" or "do it" or by asking "please." Dylan's strengths help him succeed at school.

Encourage your child to make choices and to participate in decision-making:

Joe chose his haircut. He wanted a 'Joe-Hawk' cut. Joe chooses which task he wants to do in the Kettle Korn process. He is the boss. All the employees know that when Joe wants to change and do a different task, that is his right, and they are to shift what they are doing to support this. Learning to make choices builds toward the ability to make decisions. Joe was able to participate in the decision to work in the Kettle Korn business.

Choices can be offered during any activity. For example, Dylan's Dad can ask Dylan which plant he wants to dig up.

Have the expectation that your child can get a job and be an active part of his or her community as an adult:

At Joe's final IEP meeting, his parents were told he would work in a sheltered workshop and live in a group home. But at his birth, Joe's parents consciously made a promise to give him a quality of life equal to that of his siblings. This meant he would be part of his community and to have friends. Dylan's parents are already thinking about Dylan's future job. They also want him to be an active member of his community. We'll have to wait and see where Dylan's enthusiasm takes him.

For more information about Poppin' Joe Gourmet Kettle Korn:
www.poppinjoes.com

Jo Meserve Mach is an occupational therapist. After earning her degree from the University of Kansas, she has worked for thirty-five years in both early intervention and adult services. She has specialized in the areas of sensory processing and environmental modification.

Vera Lynne Stroup-Rentier is currently completing her PhD in special education from the University of Kansas. She is an education consultant in early childhood for the Kansas State Department of Education. Stroup-Rentier specializes in foundations of self-determination for children with disabilities, family-professional partnerships, and early childhood education policies and procedures.

Mary Birdsell is a freelance photographer and a former middle school speech and theatre teacher. She has a BSE from Emporia State University and a certificate in Photo Technology from Kaw Area Technical School. In 2004, Mary received the state of Kansas award for a Teacher of Promise. She has produced more than twenty videos for Shawnee County Infant Toddler Services.

10316600R00024

Made in the USA
San Bernardino, CA
12 April 2014